# Because She's Possible

## Part I

## May H. Dalton

To order additional copies of this book, contact:
Xlibris
AU TFN: 1 800 844 927 (Toll Free inside Australia)
AU Local: 0283 108 187 (+61 2 8310 8187 from outside
Australia)
www.xlibris.com.au
Orders@Xlibris.com.au

ISBN:   Softcover      978-1-6641-0353-5
        EBook          978-1-6641-0352-8

Print information available on the last page

Rev. date: 02/25/2021

# Because She's Possible

## Part I

Written by

# May H. Dalton

For Cherri,
Wanda June,
The Watcher Tree and myself

*We are The Mother*
*We are the Empress*
*We are the protector of the Land of the Giants*

- Cherri '98

*Introduction*

On March 10<sup>th</sup> 2020, my familiar, my soul horse, my daughter, my best friend, my Cherri; passed away unexpectedly.

With her physical body, a part of myself died with her.

With her spiritual being, a part of myself was yet to be born.

In my mourning I have written, screamed, shattered, bent every direction and contemplated suicide. I've thrown my head back, cackling with glorious memories. I have been to galaxies I could never write down. I have laughed, cried, opened my arms, and closed my arms around myself, all with an expanding heart full of love. Through great turmoil, there has always been love and I thank my greatest teachers for allowing me such a big heart. Through this journey, I have re-found the name I identified with as a child through meditation. I was known as Amy until mid 2020, May is the name my truest self now returns home to.

Dearest reader, thank you for holding all the colours of my heart over Because She's Possible Parts I and II. I hope in these pages, you will feel safe in continuing on your own beautiful, ugly, terrifying and extraordinary process of becoming.

Thank you Cherri for your unwavering love and showing us humans, that if a magickal creature like you is *possible* on this Earth, anything is.

*With my love,*
*May*

*May Dalton*

I came into this world kicking and screaming like the rest of us
Donned a name of the same letters the wrong way around as Amy, for 26 years
Before remembering, I got it right when I 'misspelled' it at 5
I was a curious child, a shy teenager and an increasingly eccentric adult
I am in love with a deity
I date women
Sometimes we date women
I love all animals
Don't eat red meat
Practice white magic
Am best friends with a tree
Laugh at thunderstorms
And giggle with the moon.
I am an artist
By default by my job title
Solidified by my every action.
I carry crystals in my pockets
And I speak to my (physically) deceased Granny and Horse
I have lived my life in compartments
Before I learnt how to be free
I've cheated and I've lied
And I'm sorry.
I've bent and I've broke and I've almost died
But I forgive myself

For not knowing how to be myself
I am here now
Because I always tried
Thank you, Amy, for the wild ride
I'll let you go here
Jasmine and rosemary memorial to my ex-self
May, shed you.
Mended you.
Loved you.
This vessel that has brought me home to myself
Bold and unafraid, May
I'll run barefoot through the meadows
And talk with Wanda June
Befriend the beasts inside me, now that there are few
Let's greet the world all over
While screaming our own names
Hi,
My names May Dalton,
It's nice to meet you too

# Part I

*My favourite shade of melancholy*

I used to live life pristine
No folded down edges in this novel
Nor make-shift margins to convey my unsolicited musings
The pages were blank and my mind a jumble
A 26 year old library that never learnt of the DEWY system
Words and pages stacked to the steeples thatched rooves a frenzy to the very notion of reading backwards

I stain the pages now.

With any number of additives sometimes all at once
My pain? Take it in your sweat and tears and gritted teeth

A page ripped out.

My sadness?
I'll leave you with the page turned down so I can acknowledge you like I've never done before.
My thoughts?
Fall from my ink and stain the cracks actions can't reach.

Tear the cover off.

My new novel can have a whole new mascot that you've never heard of
She'll have a name so illusive the wind needs to blow the right direction to hear it.
She speaks to me in fables and riddles and I'm beginning to think I like it better this way
She feels more me than I have ever been

Gets the book rebound.

I will only know where I have been from the creaking spines over withered pages
Colours fading to my favorite shade of melancholy, bookmarks leaving crinkles behind and dents
My books have never been more ordered and my pages have never been more messy

I turn the page anew.

*Crimson doors*

I don't want to go through life on a meek exploration
I want to burst through its crimson doors in a dazed awe
That is, this life
A life for the living, breathing, screaming madness
A slumbering demon that sits within us all,
Either brought up in a castle or a hell
How many staircases are there until the top floor?
How many ladders must I climb until I feel like I have wings?
Can you touch the sky, or is it all around us?
Where do our spirits end and our bodies begin?
Do we teach our feet to wander or have they always known?
Did they just need to be asked?
I'd like to run full speed at the sunset.
Not for the ending,
But for what's around the darkened corner
Is there more of the moon today than last?
Or are we always just waiting for the edge,
To run closer to us

*Winter Solstice by Candlelight*

I'm smiling at trees
And I knew you wouldn't understand
I know you love them, but do you listen to them breathe?
The way they talk in the night instead of dream
The cars over the hills look like stars
And the bark of the trees is only a gleam
The raindrops are meeting the ground
And the wind is asleep
Have you sat with Mother Nature long enough
To know that it will never be long enough?
The clouds my blanket and my body a vessel
I'll journey afar, from within

Miss Magnolia
Sept. '20

*Mother Nature, I'm sorry*

Mother Nature I'm sorry
I'm so sorry we let you down
As your leaves fall like petals above me
I weep a lonely cry
For I can not help you
You are trying and you are strong
I, am small and helplessly want to protect you
But you are already burnt and crying, creaking, falling
Soot between my nails and my toes
Breeze and an off time beat through your leafless branches
Lonesome bird calls a faraway song
Shivers up my spine and not from the cold
Mother nature, I'm sorry
I will hug you as I cry until the rains return
Washing you anew
Let your little green leaves bloom
Let them burst through the grit and the rubble
May you have a beautiful rebirth
May no more harm come to you
Mother Nature, I'm sorry

Somewhere in my chest my heart is breaking and rebuilding and breaking again
I coil my body around my arms my knees to my chest and arms to my knees
My face crumpling like a paper bag in the hands of a small and reckless child
Fingernails like ravens, hair like a banshee and heart as fragile as a dove
Heavy my heart dragging around weights I did not place there, but am tasked to remove
The act of placing one foot in front of the other, requires my feet to remember I have feet
For they are so tired, I only have two weeping dinner plate eyes and a heart I push around
in a wheelbarrow
I wish for wings and immediately wonder if that's a good thing, or something you
tell the doctor.
They generally have a habit of telling me 'I'm sorry'
I generally, have a habit of slow smiling, nodding and shuffling away as I walk
In an attempt to claim it as my decision, but I never really had a choice
Did I?

*4 days. It's been. 4. Days.*

I'll be in the back booth
Sipping at my whiskey and drowning out this cruel world with heavy metal
Turn up the bass baby,
I want to hear you scream

The times humdrum come where the shadows are larger than I am
So. I will go underground where the music is louder than they are.
It's a miracle I'm not ~~dead~~ in a hospital, amazement of all that I, am in Sydney, working.
I can feel the bass through my boots bringing me closer to my familiar

You've got some nerve walking around on my turf
I am the only one welcome at this ~~funeral party~~ table
You are but a lonesome traveller
Uninvited by the host herself

Eat up sweetheart, isn't that what you said to me? Without the sunny disposition and with
an air of ~~cold hearted bitch~~ pleasure at my demise
You are kicking at my bony body while I struggle to draw breath at all.

Well now honey, I think you'll find my rage can be even more powerful than my love

I can graffiti over your heart,
I've had practice on my own

*Avoiding you, in Mary's*
14/3/20

*Suicidal dove*

Test me.
You are fighting with a Phoenix
It will be entertaining watching you squirm before I squash you
Flat.
Feel my fingers finely scrapping down your 'perfect' back
A love hate purist.
Are you using me?
Am I using you?
I think we are both as lonely as each other.
But I don't like to say it out loud.
Keep your camera, I don't want a keepsake
For fucks sake.
Leave me to be in this BnB
That no one wants to be at
I'd rather be drunk with strangers
They are far kinder to me than you ever could be
I am a worried Giant and you, a suicidal dove
You've got your wings clipped, but you're holding the scissors.

*Two souls, two eyes*
*Part 1*

There's a hole in my heart that is irreparable
I try to fill it with whiskey
But it only allows my grief to float
There's a growl in my tummy that's gone quiet
Since the moment yours went quiet
There's a silence in my ears
That's missing the sound of your constant ocean
There's a waterfall behind my eyes
That I only just realised was there so ferociously
My feet have lost all sense of direction
Since yours stopped wandering along
An ache in my heart that never used to be there
And it quivers to the touch
My eyes though.
I have your eyes.
There's something new there, and darling, I know it's you.

*Two souls, two eyes*
*Part II*

My eyes are different he tell me, staring into not one, but two souls
I feel it.
I see you, when I look at my eyes long enough.
I share my eyes now.
You, are a welcome entity.
Please, stay as long as you desire.
For you were always free.
You can saddle my wings with every breath.
I will hold you.
I will love you.
I will protect you.
Fiercely.
Forever.

*Hollow thoughts*

I don't feel quite right unless I'm half hungry
Or dehydrated
It's a small token of solidarity to your weeping bones
My bones are a hollow reminder that I lived
And you didn't.
The least I can do, is allow my bones to clink as I walk by you
A Monday afternoon symphony to my sadness in the half light
You're a daydream I dreamt for 8 years strong
Now, a pitiful, lonesome small shadow is only in my wake
It used to be 17 hands high
My shadow, is now a sad excuse for a shadow
It skulks around, but it isn't the least bit as comforting like you were
I had never been so glad to be followed by your four feet
Wherever I went, you went
I now know why you had such long legs, it was to keep up with my restless shoes
I never felt alone with you next to me, you would always end up ahead of me
I would always follow you, really
Now I walk alone.
My map no longer makes any sense, co-ordinates a mismatched tea-set from the dollar
store
No one wants this map

It's as undesirable as your ex's t-shirts
I miss the days where things felt new, comforting
A walk that was never lonesome and dreams were only
dreams, not real life nightmares I can not out-run
Now, I lose track if I am awake or asleep
For a reality without you,
Is just as painful.

*Making wishes on bird bones*

Arriving home from the grocery store
I find myself making wishes on bird bones
Wrist deep in carving the chicken
That I don't want to eat
And I know I should eat
Because that's one of the things keeping us humans alive and so on
In slapping together my thoughts with all about internal fury
I make my way out to dine with the bees
And remember that we are all two of the same
And maybe, its not so bad really?
And I do so, leaving my Tony Biancos on the doorstep
Slipping into my usual sensibilities of fresh air and mantras
Sing-a-long songs of the evening bird parade
A tune to my mandatory well-being picnic
But its ok.
And it is ok
That it's been a bad day
For tomorrow is new
And the sky will be blue
And damn it
You tried.

*Aromatherapy and cults*

Sitting by the fire
Sewing on buttons to 70's rock
I wait to see if this day will make anymore sense the longer I sit on it
It doesn't.
The girls face in the shop yesterday was worn in a way that everything sounded expensive
And she certainly wouldn't take your phone call
Norwood snobs.
Maybe, if I get high at the end of my day, it will make all the other days make sense
I'm not sure.
But I am damn going to buy another candle and trial by aromatherapy and cults.
The ghost that lives in the kitchen was quieter than usual today
No matter how much I dared
Did you know
I use sage on myself, more than I do the ghosts
Funny that.
It's not the outside world that's off balance
It's all the internal ones, that are.

Matriarch '21

I cover it up with make-up
Nothing.
Change my clothes.
Nope, still there.
Pour a gin.
Down a gin.
Go outside. Shake.
Better.

*- Nothing can cleanse like you, Mother Nature*

*Tired*

I'm getting tired
Of getting dressed in accordance to what dress is easiest to hitch-up for the gynecologist
Or leaving my lacey underwear in the draw, hoping there's space in my hand bag for the
'just in case' maxi-pad
I'm getting tired
Of making, and un-making and re-making plans based on the unscheduled
whims of my uterus
I'm tired
Of getting high
And staying high
On some sort of perscription concoction or another
I'm tired of talking about it
I'm tired of invisible barbed wire tightening around my abdomen – in public or otherwise
And when I say 'tired'
I don't mean
Get some more beauty sleep, sleep a little longer, deeper, sleep in, dear
No.
I mean I'm exhausted
From carrying a wire fence around my body
A stone in my heart
And an encyclopedia at the forefront of my brain
Whatever this feeling is,
I hardly remember the mild inconvenience that was 'tired'
And this,

This.
This is nothing like it.

*Hindsight*

If I told you stories on chronological order
It wouldn't be accurate
To how life works.
You don't understand your life, in order
It's a jumbled, tumbled hindsight that no one warns you about
The course curriculum that will be in no particular order, or duration for that matter
Maybe some courses aren't even available to you.
Maybe, you need to do some of the classes more than once
More than once
More than once
One thing you most certainly are guaranteed,
You will not understand yourself truly, perhaps until years after you've sat your test

Beautiful
MESS

8th Jan
'21

*Perpetual mourning*

I couldn't dead-head the hydrangeas this year
They are too close to you
Even an act of plant violence within 50 meters of you feels wrong
Except for the flowers I used to weave you a blanket
The dead flowers now droop so low in solidarity
I'd rather them stay in perpetual mourning

*Ode to suburban norms:*

Dear suburban pavement,
I can so walk on you barefoot
Even though the other orangutan's look at me funny
Shoes are a new invention
Feet aren't.
And why yes,
Those are my nipples shinning through my clean white t-shirt
What business is it of yours?
There are some cows in the backyard that sometimes moo so loudly, they keep me up at night
But they are a damn sight easier than two children and a husband I don't like
My fences are wonky
But they sure are stronger than your white pickets I promise
The hours I work are irregular, but I enjoy making art much more than I can ever explain to you
While you're out busy counting the money you slave to earn, only to throw it on a lifestyle
~~you didn't even choose~~ I mean - the one you just went along with
Not making hard choices,
Is still a choice
Complaining about things you can actually control, isn't it tiresome?
More tiresome, I imagine
Than deflecting strange looks from the other orangutan's

*Summertime girlfriend*

I am her Summertime girlfriend
A flicker of reds and oranges
Dancing across her wrought iron bed
A nudist daydream in a Newtown BnB
A drunken midnight confession in my then suburban home
The three sudden kisses in the Blue Mountains
Sparkled dress up's to salsa dance in the city
We were always fated
Equally red lips, bound to collide and stay stuck
You are, and were always, the potion I wanted to sip
The intrigue that wouldn't leave my mind
A question unasked on curious, un-moving lips
Answered only, when my lips found yours with intent
My body, chasing after

*Tulips*

I see you
Holding up the walls with your bare hands
Just so they have something to do other than rip my clothes apart
I too, am a frozen Wallflower
Ass parked firmly to the doorframe as a school-girl, before she knew she liked girls
Did you feel the subtle tug at your shirt like I did?
When did you first start to notice how plump a woman's lips become when they are turned on?
Two tulips parting together in an Autumn breeze
I remember the first time I started watching your mouth when you talked
Wishing I was each word being pressed together out of your lips
A knowing then what I know now
A fire and a Hurricane, can not be tamed

*Letters to Cherri,*

I miss you.
'I miss you' isn't big enough for how I really feel about you.
I feel, everything about you.
Hair. Dust. The essence of stardust.
The way you would sigh into my hug, wrapping your head around my shoulder. Squeezing me. Steadying. Flying. Breathing. Balancing.
Being.

*An ode to grief*

I'm trying to fill myself up with wishes
But there's a bottomless hole I can never reach
I scream and I curse I burst and I cry
I think that I'll die
And I don't.
You catch me as I fall, cradled rocking and all
Holding my bones in place, safe
Keep me together, it's now or never
I can't stand up straight, I think I might break
Down.
Now.
Where do you go from here?
We try to joke and to laugh, it feels too formal
My body is still weak at the knees
Someone please help me, tell me I'm dreaming
Please?
Back to the bottle, I know you're trouble
But the truth is, it could be worse dear
For now that she's gone, it's a miracle that I am here.

*Familiar: Sweet pea promises*

You're lying in the meadows you used to run and play in
Softly, you make the winds do your bidding
They oblige to your wishes
You speak to me through my chest now
A pocket sized version of yourself treads lightly on my aorta
Reminding me I am alive
And therefore you are
Sweet peas are blooming above you
I know they bloom for you alone
The sun comes out for you
The moon, bows to your beauty
And rainbows dreamt about being so bright
You fill me with a love so radiant the neighbors will need sunglasses
I promise I will be generous with this light
I'll give it to those we love
I'll keep some for us, you, and me, both
I won't mistreat myself
For I would never harm you.
Your sunshine heart will keep beating
And we will not fear the dark.

*Familiar: Wander with me*

There's something eerily poetic in walking
By your place of rest
Barefoot
How else would I really?
My feet, antenna to your always-honest wisdom
An aura felt
Far before I reach you
White magnet, nickering, lavender scented force field
You fill my every sense
From the ground-up
A shiver.
The good kind
The one where I can feel your spirit
Inside me
The warm sunshine hug
From you
To me,
Inside me
Your body may rest
But your soul,
Has always, and will always, wander with me
With this forest
In the very fiber of the universe

Spencer 4     Sept.
              '20

*My dogs scared of the bathroom*

My dog's scared of the bathroom
And I don't blame him
All sorts of things get cleaned in here
The angst of a long day
Egos
Former selves
Pubic hair trimmed
Beards shaved clean off
Orgasams have been had loudly
Chemicals used
To wash away evidence of anything at all
One time,
After her physical death
Cherri gave me one of her memories so painful,
I screamed in the bathtub
Sometimes no amount of lavender is enough
Or that time
I used the bath mat like a lazy Susan
An invention required of doubled over endometriosis
My dogs afraid of the bathroom
And I don't blame him
Sometimes, I am too

*Don't pretend to know my name*

Don't call me on your restricted numbers
A disrespect to knowing my own
In fact, even better
Leave me alone.
Leave me to my own devices
Yours wouldn't suit me anyway I'm sure
Delete my number and forget I ever owned a phone
I prefer not to use it anyway
Call me by my name or don't call me at all
Disconnection error: Wavelength not compatible

*Girl*

"Watch out for the girl behind you"
The dear old couple in the supermarket said
Gesturing to me in the condiments isle
Girl.
A pig tailed vision of innocence springs to my mind
And the fresh scent of linen in my nose
Girl.
So freshly dressed in her Sunday best
A giggly smile at the boys
More shy than sly
Pre-monster teen
Girl.
A sundress in any weather
Lip-gloss too far around her lips
Sparkles in her hair
And every colour polish on her tippy toes
Girl.
Best friends to everyone
And no one she will know forever
Even after we pinky swear it so in the playground
A hopscotch hope reality won't yet touch
Girl.
So far away and right beside me
Reverting to my girlhood wandering and tree talking
Today,
Is a perfect day to be called 'Girl'
Not as a dismissal to my womanhood, but a declaration of

I am so comfortable in my womanhood, my girlhood is here too
Laugh a cackle, half way skipping through the garden
Hair glowing in the sunlight
Dirt between my bare toes
Falling over brambles just to pick the fruit
A life so sweet,
It was worth running through thorns for

At the top of the driveway
A sight for sore hippies
Poncho: Multi-coloured
Hair: Green and red
In front of a tree I talk with
Crystals
A candle
And a singing bowel
Welcome,
To the pine forest
- *It's not a cult, but why would you want to leave?*

*Night swimming*

I look at the ceiling
A clatter of my own laugher
Screaming at my rain washed insides
I, a clamor to my clicking armor as it falls around my feet
You, a portrait of a boy so aquiver with big ideas
I want to throw you into your own imagination
So you can swim around in your own aptitude
I can't see the ceiling all I see are stars
And my darling, tonight they shine for me and you

*Horse whisperer*

There's a black horse
Rearing up on it's hind legs
A neigh and a buck
Flared nostrils and a wild mane
Ears back, flat
Neck up, guard up
I, a small steady to your manic mind
Fear is swimming in the horses eyes
My pains eyes
Panicking parallel
The only notion to calm down
A slow and desolate 'whooah'
Doltish tones fallen on scared ears
Why should a 'whoah' be trusted
When full well,
There is panic for a reason
Many, no doubt
But here we are.
The black stallion
And the whisperer
Trying ever so hard
To allow calm, compassion
To rise against
Anxious rage

*The reason my beret slouches - Part I*

I sit in overcast sunlight
Cider in hand. Beret worn at a slouch.
Music overhead
A perfect red-lip
You would never know
I picked my self off the literal floor today.
10/10 pain. Doubled-over. Knife wounds to the gut.
You would never know from how I look
Maybe just a hint when I answer 'You too' to 'Enjoy your meal!'.
Hands shake as I eat.
Don't want to eat.
Do it anyway.
Sun in my eye, don't cry. Sit up straight. Drink too much. Show no weakness. Don't be a fool. Keep your plans. Don't be unreliable. Keep your trouble under your hat. Pull it tighter over your face. Don't wait. Post-haste. Day-drunk just to wear my face on straight.

*The reason my beret slouches - Part II*

So I try and hide your feelings
Like a disobedient - I mean – childwithalotoffeelings child
Determined to make up all the ill in my wake
Even though it's not my fault.
You feel it's your fault.
It's your body, your disobedient body – I mean – bodywithalotoffeelingsbody
So instead,
I sit.
In quiet
They wont tell from the look on my face
That it's because of my supernatural grace

*Alone in public*

I'll be drinking alone in the back booth
Not because I'm lonely
But because I enjoy being alone in public
I enjoy being alone in public because I get to watch you
When I'm alone in public
You don't think I see you
Because I'm busy 'being lonely'
But, I'm not
I'm busy putting my thoughts into line
My lines into poetry
And my poetry back to you
The public.
So that,
Is why I like sitting alone
Sitting with myself, rather
In public
To avoid you short term
So you can hear me talking about you long term
Where maybe
Just maybe
You will be sitting alone with yourself long enough
To hear
Not to listen
But to hear
I wonder
When's the last time you sat with yourself?
Not out of lonely necessity
But for utter lust to do so
To listen to yourself
Your own narrative unfolding, a cinema before you

For you
About you
Because of you

*Food for thought*

To the teenager sitting across from me:
Your food is less fascinating than your friend, I'm sure.
So, why are you taking more photos of plates full?
Florescent light lighting up your millennial insecurities
Flash. Flash.
Oh!
Change that angle, make your lunch a STAR
How many likes on Instagram you 'achieve' is disproportionate to your worth
How long, until you know this I wonder?
How many memory full iPhone's until you will ever know.
Technology is a charade.
A front.
Imaginary.
And your friendships will be too, unless you pay more attention to her, than your food.

*This is Australia 2020*

I see you
Stocking your trolley's high like mine
A nod to a stranger, you can't see my smile behind my mask in isle four
'This is Australia' blares from the crackly overhead speaker as I leave the bottle-o
Smell of marijuana in the air wafts faintly through the car-park
And I marvel at the sights and smells that are
This sunburnt land in a heat turned up everything feels sticky
Return to the car a sanctuary clean
Mask hanging in the coat hook behind me
This is Australia
This is as resilient as it comes
Batten down the hatches and pour yourself a drink
Settle in for the week
Hibernation a lonely hope until it's safe again to dance

*Invisibility cloak*

I see your gender and I see your identity
Standing in the grocery store line hoping that nobody sees me
Red coat merely to cover myself up today
I spy
Your tree tattoo and I make a note that it's a good sign
I'm choking on my own tongue too fat for sitting between my teeth
It surprises us both when I open my nearly mute mouth
'I love your tree tattoo' I say
'I'm getting one there myself there soon' A nodding reassuring smile to the stranger
'Oh! Thank you!' The kind, shy, I assume transgender cashier replies
We talk for a little while and I leave smiling
With a tear in my eye
Knowing that I am a good person
Even when I started this same day
Wanting to end it.

*First date, an observation*

I'm watching you
New lovers
Who aren't yet lovers
You're not sitting close enough to have slept with one another yet
But you're not far enough away that you don't want to...
She asks a lot of questions, so he doesn't have to
But she isn't committed enough to remove her sunglasses from her head yet
He's on his phone occasionally
I wonder if it's because she's swearing a lot
Or maybe, he's a jerk and she needs to swear to be heard
No,
She's definitely swearing a lot.
I wonder if this is their first date
I assume so.
I wonder if they've noticed me listening in on their conversations yet
Don't think so
They are too busy trying to impress one another
Definitely a first date
Or a last date
She made a wedding joke.
Back-peddle.
Now they are talking about their family. Oh dear.
I wonder
If they will know each other in a year from now
A month from now
A week from now

I wonder,
But the thought slips off me like lace
For I am not involved
And in the nicest way possible,
I don't care.

The Watcher Nov '20

*A restless child*

'Come and sit down with me' says the tree
Sit down?! HA! Sitting down is no match for my restless child's legs.
A scoff at the very notion of 'sitting down'
Where's the use in that?

'Take a break my dear' the woman thinks she hears the branches coo…
Convinced, if but briefly, that sitting still could be an idea worth entertaining
A quick sit and then a nagging inner voice,
Off up again to the rest of the day

'Hello, my equal' The Watching Tree says boldly to the Newborn Empress
A nod to the fresh flowers laid at her roots, followed by a small redhead in full lotus
The cosmic collision of wise old spirits
Reattaching

This is it.
All that we ought to be in search for
An inner peace so deep, you wonder how you've been wandering around so empty without it all your former lives
But none of that matters here, you're free

I am taking a holiday,
They'll say
Pina colada, skinny dipping
Island Queen
No.
I am going inwards honey
Right here.
Tree hugging, circle spinning
Forest Empress

*Hymn for her majesty*

Across the way and down the pasture
Lived a girl free from master
Two in a hammock
Douse in laughter
Bottom of the garden
Or front rather
'Neath the blue wren a feather
Roses blooming in this weather
Fresh air a quiver
Happy shiver
Now is the time to be really giving
Look out love; I think you're living
Up and down a path well driven
Lies a truth that's rarely given
Sits a girl who sees as well
With the past and present realms
Soothing voice to those who dwell
Past the tree, purple as it is green
Bring your flowers, bended knee
Make your circle as wide as narrow
Worries taken, Father sparrow
Round the scared tree we live
At your majesty, we will give

Part I ♥

*We were all born with a box of matches in our hands*

I've been holding my breath for a while now
Say, 17 years now?
Moving my way through life like everybody else
Pickett fence, suffragette
Made a fool out of a diamond-neck
Doing all the right things for society, forget you and me
We are but a wheel in a far too large machine
I didn't think I could stop it turning
Let alone change it's direction
I, at the helm of my own life
Red hair a wave behind me
Them, a distant far off sea
I am out in the open waters of my own making
Not stuck in your ponds or streams
For my screams you see, if used consistently
Caused me, to move into a different life
Ones wildest dreams come true
But there is a catch Fairy Godmother, see?
First, you must blow up life, as you know it, entirely
And further still,
You must be the one to light the fuse
To risk it all
On a chance at true happiness that you can't yet picture
Forgive me here, when I play the devil
But I would rather choose the life of arson
If it means happiness for the rest of my eternity

Dragonflies were having sex through the air
And I watched in awe at their fleeting copulation
Admiring a 24hour festival of sex and death

Hours passing and heart quickening
A walk down dim lit hallway, nude and beckoning
Let the forest watch us in our loving making

I,
Reborn again in our galaxies passing
We dip in and dive out, a serpent rising
Floating through stratospheres
You,
A heart so connected to each other
I inhale you and exhale you, writhing
A tantric heartbeat tethering
We,
A little death, revitalising
God and Goddess, immortalising
Green and pinks are blinding

Heart meridian warm and winding
New universes are here for the finding
Together connected in new entwining

Admiring the freedom in space travel
A view, while bent backwards in ecstasy
The continuum expanding and eclipsing

The Horned God has claimed his Goddess
In the name of sex and death

*I am the forest and the forest is me*

This is not a tattoo
This is an amulet
What is on the inside
Is now on the outside
I am the forest and the forest is me
I feel now with my Third Eye
I understand from my core
Out through my feet
Life is a balance
And balance is life
I am not afraid of the forest
For she is not afraid of me
We inhale
And we exhale as one
I am the forest
And the forest is me

*Thank you*

Thank you to my darling partner in the universe, Travis. You have held me in my darkest hours, with the same love, adoration and respect as my brightest ones. I love you to the Pleiades and back.

My Mother and Father, thank you for encouraging me to let out my heart, even and especially, when I have been afraid of it. I am thankful everyday to have you both as parents.

My publishing company, thank you for allowing a larger platform so that this book may fall into the hands of whomever needs to hold it and be held by it.

Thank you dear reader for receiving poems closest to my heart.

*With love,*
*May*

Other titles by May Dalton
Under her previous name, Amy Heather

*Phoenix*

*Wildling*

Social media:

*Instagram*
*@mayh.dalton_*

May H. Dalton, lives in South Australia with her fiancé Travis, dog Spencer and cat Makoto.

She works as a professional model of 9 years and counting, making art with her body with fluid expression.

She began writing after an abusive relationship as a form of healing and strongly encourages others to speak their truths in whichever format sits with ones soul.

Today, May walks barefoot with the forest, knows the trees by name and continues on her inner exploration daily.

May and Travis hope to adopt a horse or two in continual honor of the horse that saved May's life.

Cover art and artist portrait
taken by
Travis Langs
*Social media*
*Instagram*
*@travis.langs*